I0181366

A VISIT TO DAMANHUR

DAILY LIFE, THOUGHTS AND HISTORY OF A COMMUNITY OF DREAMERS

DAMANHUR

A VISIT TO DAMANHUR

by Formica Coriandolo (Angela Toninelli)
and Stambecco Pesco (Silvio Palombo)

ISBN: 978-88-941185-0-6

Devodama srl, Vidracco (TO), Italy

Printed in September 2015

Formica Coriandolo (Angela Toninelli) is the coordinator of the Public Relations office of Damanhur, Federation of Communities. Stambecco Pesco (Silvio Palombo), writer, is the author of *La mia Damanhur* (Altri Paraggi).

CONTENTS

DAMANHUR
tel.+39.0124.512226
www.damanhur.it
Federazione di Comunità

DAMANHUR, FEDERATION OF COMMUNITIES

Damanhur is a Federation of spiritual communities located in the north Piedmont region of Italy, between Turin and Aosta. It spans an area with a 15-kilometer radius centered in the Valchiusella, a valley that is still green and clean. Here, the citizens of Damanhur have created a multilingual society open to exchanges with the local people and with cultures from all over the world. Damanhurians have animal and plant names, as a symbol of union with nature.

Damanhur was founded in 1975, inspired by Falco Tarassaco, Oberto Airaudi (1950-2013). His illuminated and pragmatic vision gave rise to a community based on solidarity, love, spirituality and respect for the environment, so much so as to obtain recognition in 2005 as a model for a sustainable society by the Global Human Settlements Forum of the United Nations.

Damanhur welcomes thousands of visitors every year and attracts the interest of scholars and researchers from all over the world in the fields of social sciences, art, spirituality and environmental sustainability.

In Damanhurian philosophy, which inspires life in the communities of the Federation, positive thinking, valuing diversity, inner change as a strategy to get out of our usual habits, are all fundamental aspects of life.

Damanhur is an experience of researching life's profound values, in every aspect. In 40 years, Damanhurians have created initiatives in the fields of labor, politics, culture, education, art and research in the subtle energies that guide the universe.

The spiritual pathway, called the School of Meditation, guides every Damanhurian in self-exploration and seeking the meanings of existence, including through the study of ancient magical traditions and celebrations of the rhythms of nature. Along this path, everyone learns to develop their own talents and refine their limitations, helping others to do the same.

Respect for the environment is one of the foundations of the Damanhurian way of thinking. Damanhurians cultivate the earth and raise animals organically, renovate and construct buildings according to eco-building criteria, and they have developed companies that plan and install renewable energy systems. They also favor natural methods of healing and a holistic vision of medicine.

Seeking a better integration between human beings and the environment comes about through giving attention to the most low-impact choices possible, as well as through researching the most advanced technological solutions.

In the Damanhurian vision, technology, when properly understood and used, is a valuable ally in the defense of health and nature.

Respect for the environment is something that goes beyond an ecologist vision. It also means recognizing the existence of self-aware and sensitive life in the plant world, as well as in the animal kingdom, and seeking contact with the intelligent beings who inhabit this universe.

One of the results of this approach is the experience in the field of plant communication, whose most well known expression is the "Music of the Plants," which makes it possible to hold concerts where the musicians are trees, plants and human beings, playing music together.

The achievement for which Damanhur is most well known is the Temples of Humankind, an underground complex excavated entirely by hand in the heart of the mountain, decorated with mosaics, stained glass, sculptures, wall paintings and works of art dedicated to the awakening of the divine spark present in every human being. The Temples are visited each year by thousands of people.

Damanhur has centers, organizations and contacts in many cities in Italy, Europe and around the world. You can come visit any time of the year, attend courses and seminars, and learn about Falco Tarassaco's philosophy and way of thinking.

Welcome to this virtual visit to Damanhur, Federation of Communities.

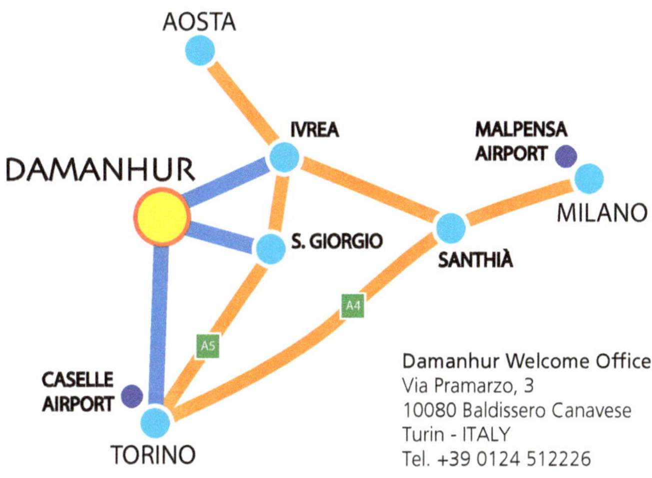

DAMANHURIAN COMMUNITIES

LIVING TOGETHER

Damanhur is home to about 600 people: resident citizens in the communities of the Federation, "temporary" citizens and children. About 400 more people live nearby, many of them from different countries. Those who have bought houses to live near Damanhur are called "non-resident" citizens.

Damanhurian citizens come from diverse backgrounds from a social, cultural and geographic perspective. Some had come to Damanhur when they were very young, and others have done so at an older age. The primary spoken language is Italian, although there are many people whose mother languages are English, German, Dutch, Croatian, Norwegian and Spanish.

Even the individual pathways for coming to Damanhur are quite diverse. Many have moved near the communities for spiritual motivations, others for environmental ones, and still others are attracted by the research being done here in education or sustainability, and so on. Regardless of the reasons, anyone who arrives at Damanhur is sure to discover many aspects of life experience here.

Living in community with others from diverse backgrounds brings with it opportunities for tremendous enrichment.

You can come to Damanhur whisked away by a mystical idea, fascinated by the social dimension, determined to defend nature, or for many other reasons that will be harmonized with the motivations of others, once you are here. Some people arrive with the idea of making a lifetime choice.

The challenge of harmonious coexistence among so many people from different cultures is fascinating. It requires constant adaptation and a robust sense of humor! Many ingredients blend together to create a stable community that is in continuous evolution, capable of renewing itself and able to create a strong sense of overall cohesion. All of these things are important, but the most fundamental ones are: love, respect and reciprocal solidarity.

The awareness that everyone can offer something unique and valuable to others, that we are all part of a single essence that is one family called Humanity: this is the flame that warms and connects the hearts of all Damanhurians. For this reason, the Four Pillars of Damanhur—that is, the four main areas of experience and research—have the objective to provide useful tools for knowing ourselves and each other, giving space to the expression of individual characteristics and talents. The Social Pillar is the area that coordinates the community and political aspects of Damanhurian life.

For more information about **Damanhur** and visits to the communities, you may contact **Damanhur Welcome & University** at Damjl, in Baldissero Canavese, Italy. **www.damanhur.org - Tel. +39 0124 512226**.

DAMANHURIAN CITIZENS

You can become a citizen of Damanhur, choosing from different formulas.

Citizens who choose the communitarian formula, also known as "resident citizens," reside in large houses shared by nucleo families of between about 15 and 25 people. Couples, couples with children, singles, youth and the elderly live in the same dwelling to allow for the exchange of experiences among various age groups. Everyone has their own private space and shares common areas with others, such as the kitchen, living room, and rooms dedicated to meeting together.

Sharing is extended in many aspects of daily life and occurs on many occasions: during the weekly meetings, where we give and receive support and personal feedback, make decisions and develop projects; in the administration of the community; when handling daily expenses for food, rent, maintenance and management of the house and the land, and so on; also in the distribution of roles that are useful to help maintain a high quality of life.

"Resident Citizens" elect their representatives in the roles that manage various responsibilities. Those with "resident citizenship" also participate in and support the activities of the associations that take care of various aspects of community life.

Like the resident citizens, non-resident citizens participate in all spiritual, artistic and research activities. The majority of them live in the Canavese zone, which are the neighboring areas of the various communities. There are numerous private homes of non-resident citizens, town apartments and farmsteads, where these citizens live alone or with their families, sometimes even creating small community groups.

Some of the non-resident citizens participate daily in the practical activities of the community, while others do so in different moments, staying connected with the communities for which they feel a strong affinity.

There are also non-residents who live in distant cities, in Italy and around the world, who come to Damanhur several times a year and participate, depending on the distance involved and their personal commitments. Many of them are engaged in the creation and management of Damanhur Embassies and Centers, where Damanhur instructors go to offer courses, conferences and seminars.

TEMPORARY CITIZENS

For those who are curious about Damanhur and simply want to have an experience as a Damanhur citizen for three months, we have created temporary citizenship through the New Life program. In this program, you are integrated into a nucleo community and participate in the daily life of citizens. At the same time, you will attend classes on Damanhurian philosophy, history and spirituality as well as the Italian language. It is an opportunity to receive the knowledge that Falco Tarassaco passed on to us.

New Life temporary citizens are unlike those who spend time at Damanhur as guests, staying in dedicated facilities and attending programs organized by Damanhur Welcome & University. New Life citizens get to have a perspective from inside the Damanhur experience.

During the three months, every New Life participant stays in at least two different nucleo communities in order to connect with various people and get to know different ways of being together.

At the end of three months, temporary citizens return to their places of origin or, if they wish, they may enter into a trial period to become Damanhurian resident citizens.

Welcoming temporary citizens is also a wonderful experience for Damanhurians who have lived in community for years. It's an opportunity to encounter different languages and cultures, have a dialogue about the most everyday aspects like cooking, to the more profound ones like the education of children, respect for the environment and spirituality. This is a source of enrichment for all of us.

For more information about the **New Life program – temporary citizenship**, you may visit to **www.damanhur.org/new-citizens**

QUALITY OF LIFE

During Damanhur's 40-year history, the citizens' quality of life has improved dramatically. Today, the community has many hundreds of acres of land, dozens of eco-friendly homes, abundant services and facilities that can accommodate citizens and guests, vital businesses, organic farming, renewable energy in every community, the Damanhur School for children, a center for integrative medicine and many other aspects that make life rich and varied.

Solidarity, sharing and the industriousness of Damanhurians are the values that have enabled this richness to grow for the benefit of all.

At Damanhur, supporting those in difficulty is a core value, as well as supporting the elderly, children and pregnant women. Every citizen is guaranteed a high standard of care, regardless of the type of activity that he carries out or the state assistance he receives.

The entire community supports children in their studies, because education is valued and supported by everyone.

The health care system offers many possibilities and allows everyone to choose how to care for themselves. Alongside traditional Damanhurian therapies—pranatherapy, gentle therapies, natural medicine, to name a few—there is a clinic where several doctors work (the majority of whom are Damanhur citizens) and where many specialized services are provided for Damanhurians, as well as patients from nearby towns.

ELECTED BODIES

The political system in the Federation of Communities is inspired by the principles of the Constitution of Damanhur. All the roles of representation that comprise this system are chosen through elections.

Every six months, the citizens vote for the two King Guides, the highest office in the social sector. The King Guides are responsible for coordinating the activities and development of the entire Federation.

In every nucleo community, elections are held once a year for the caponucleo, or regent. This is the person who coordinates community life from the perspective of social relationships, organization and the implementation of various community projects. Also, given the vastness of Damanhur, in each distinct area where several nucleo communities are grouped together and identified as a region, a Captain is elected yearly by members of those various communities.

Each year, the College of Justice is elected as well. Their task is to ensure that the principles of the Constitution are respected, disputes between citizens are resolved, and the work of the various roles and institutions are verified.

CONSTITUTION

The Constitution of Damanhur contains the fundamental principles that are the basis of life in the Federation of Communities.

Among these principles, there are: positive thinking about others, continuous inner transformation, solidarity and respect for all citizens, always giving someone another chance, and caretaking the environment and all forms of life.

The Constitution of Damanhur was made to evolve over time, according to a precise philosophical vision: to create a community that can sustain itself with ever-increasing individual awareness, with less and less need for laws and regulations.

The first draft of the Constitution was written in 1981, and it contained more than 130 articles. After many iterations, the current version is only 15 articles.

The Constitution bans smoking, drug use and any form of excess behavior that can harm ourselves and others. Damanhurians abide by these guidelines as a lifestyle choice, and all guests who visit Damanhur are asked to respect these rules while present here.

THE EDUCATION OF CHILDREN

At Damanhur, education is considered to be an opportunity for intellectual, social, ethical and spiritual growth—not just for children, but for educators, teachers, parents... and the entire Damanhur family!

The diversity of cultures and nationalities at Damanhur contributes to the richness of the educational environment. For both children and adults in the community, it expands our capacity to think creatively and welcome new ideas. Children are educated from an early age to be responsible individuals and citizens of the world who are capable of determining their own future. At 18 years of age, or even a few years before if they have the prerequisites, Damanhur youth can choose whether to continue living in a nucleo community with their parents or have other experiences. For example, one option is participation in a project called Casa Ragazzi, a community run by Damanhurian youth from 15 years to 23 years of age.

THE DAMANHUR SCHOOL

The Damanhur School was founded in 1985 by a group of parents whose vision was to directly guide the education of their children.

The Damanhur Education organization created the school to include curriculum that aligns with all the programs of the Italian educational ministry. This government educational institute provides verification and annual final exams for the students.

Children are central in Damanhur's educational vision. Beyond the standard Italian curriculum, there is an abundance of activities that give space for self-expression, from having contact with nature to practical experimentation in many fields, for example, in the arts and ecology.

Children often work together in classes with different age groups represented. This fosters skills and provides mutual support. Each group has an educator as a reference person who collaborates with all the other teachers.

Students travel together with their teachers, whenever possible, to many historical sites in Italy and in the world, so they gain practical knowledge of what they are learning in school, having a direct experience of what would otherwise remain virtual.

They get to know the world in this way and gain experiences in autonomy.

The school is actively involved in environmental awareness and international solidarity campaigns. For example, the students offered support for the construction of a school on Mancarroncito, an island in Nicaragua.

They have also been in contact with many Greenpeace activists, visiting the Rainbow Warrior ship while it was docked in Genova, Italy.

YOUTH COMMUNITY

In 2007, a group of adolescent Damanhur children created the Milte nucleo community, also called Casa Ragazzi. With participation from youth between the ages of 15 to 23, they took on the experiment of living together without adults, with a great sense of responsibility and autonomy. In doing so, they learned about mutual support and personal responsibility. Independent of their parents, they managed all aspects of daily life: shopping, cooking, cleaning, budgeting, and so on.

The main house rule at Casa Ragazzi is that, in addition to managing all of the chores and responsibilities, it is essential for each student to maintain a good academic standing in their school. If their performance is insufficient, the youth return to the nucleo community where their parents live; however, the children's support for one another makes this occurrence extremely rare.

Federazione di

ECONOMY AND WORK

The Damanhurian economic system reconciles free enterprise with solidarity and sharing, with the aim of creating individual and collective wealth. This system has created the base for what has become a great collective wealth over time.

This includes land and houses, schools and services, works of art and gardens, woods and meeting spaces, as well as health and wellness services.

This quality of life revitalizes the geographic areas where Damanhurian settlements are located.

All residents of these areas can enjoy the services and activities, alongside the citizens of Damanhur. From the time that the community was founded until today, the economic structure of Damanhur has changed many times. During the first 10 years, citizens chose to share their individual income by putting it into a common fund that was used to purchase land and houses. This fund made it possible to create the basis for community development and to initiate work on the Temples of Humankind. After this first essential phase, the citizens chose to return to managing their own economic resources. In this way, every person had an incentive to express his or her individual potential supported by the availability of personal economic resources.

Today, each community is administered like a real family, where those who work participate in covering costs, supporting those in need.
According to the possibilities of each person, everyone participates in supporting the objectives of the Federation, such as the Damanhur School, the Temples of Humankind, etc.
Damanhurians created a housing cooperative called Atalji in order to have collective ownership of all of the Federation's property assets. This patrimony has grown over time through Atalji's investments—acquiring new land and most of all renovating old houses—and also through contribution in the form of shares held by its members, who are the citizens themselves. Every citizen can withdraw their shares if they decide to leave the citizenship, or if they have an unexpected necessity.

THE "CREDITO"

The "Credito" is Damanhur's complementary currency system. The community's objective in creating this coinage was to develop a new form of economy based on the ethical values of cooperation and solidarity.

The "Credito" is a return to the use of money in its original meaning: as a means to facilitate exchange, based on an agreement between those involved.

The word "Credito" (credit) reminds us that money is a tool through which we grant trust. This currency system raises the concept of money to a more noble status. It is not considered a goal in and of itself, but rather a functional tool for exchange between people.

In technical terms, the "Credito" is a functional account unit, active in a predetermined and predefined circuit. Today, the "Credito" has the same value as the Euro. In compliance with Italian law and administrative obligations, purchases from all economic activities present in Damanhur provide for and favor the circulation of "Credito" as a system of internal exchange.

Upon arrival at Damanhur, it is possible for all guests and friends to convert Euro currency at Damanhur Welcome & University or in the designated change machines located around the main areas. "Credito" that are unused may be reconverted into Euro at any time.

You may find **machines for changing Euros to "Credito" currency** at **Damjl**, under the portico along the front parking lot, and at **Damanhur Crea**.

IN CIVIL SOCIETY

Damanhur is a demonstration that new forms of society are possible and achievable. This is an important step toward the creation of a new social, economic, human and cultural equilibrium. For Damanhurians, living in community means being open to the world, being part of a social and political system that is capable of responding to the needs of citizens, with a sense of service to society.

In 2005, Damanhur received recognition as a model for a sustainable society from the Global Human Settlements Forum of the United Nations (UN). This award recognizes Damanhur's active engagement in offering our experience in service to others.

Since 1980, when Damanhurians created the first settlements in Baldissero Canavese, Vidracco, and Cuceglio, Italy, they have participated in local, provincial and regional elections through the political movement "Con Te, per il Paese," (With you, for the country). Taking on active commitments in the local area is considered to be one of the key prerequisites to being a socially active community.

Also, it is important to create political and legislative spaces that protect and regulate life in small and large communities such as Damanhur and many other ecovillages, which have much to say and to offer to the society where they are located.

AIB DAMANHUR
ROSSA
Associazione Protezione Civile
DAMANHUR
DAMANHUR

On the national Italian level, Damanhur supports submitting a law on intentional communities to Parliament aimed at recognizing "community" as a status for groups that comply with a set of parameters with respect to transparency, social structure and longevity.

From the earliest years of Damanhur, its citizens have been engaged in volunteering: in regional fire-fighting teams, for emergency aid teams, the Italian Red Cross and the Fire Brigade. Many Damanhurians have participated in humanitarian interventions, such as "Rainbow Mission" in Albania, helping refugees from Kosovo, assisting with emergency aid after the Sri Lanka tsunami in 2004 and after the earthquake of L'Aquila in 2009, and on many other occasions in the Piedmont region and around Italy.

A SUSTAINABLE WAY OF LIFE

SELF-SUFFICIENCY AND RESPECT FOR THE ENVIRONMENT

Damanhur's ecological vision, beyond cultivating respect for nature, is also a way to reawaken the awareness of how we as human beings are deeply united with every element of life around us.

The base of our community experience exists in a network of ethical, cultural and spiritual values. These values create the foundation of an economic system that both supports the citizens of Damanhur and serves as a local resource through supply chains that allow for the circulation of wealth among local business activities.

At Damanhur, even the concept of peace is related to global sustainability. Peace is not only seen as the absence of conflict but also as creating the conditions for well-being in all areas of the world through valuing local resources, so that all peoples may live on their own lands, in happiness and in harmony with the ecosystem around them, without depending on outside resources.

Damanhur moves in the direction of complete self-sufficiency for many reasons: to acquire and develop the widest possible range of skills (from simple personal skills to the great competencies of specialized companies), to ensure the high quality of its products, and to be able to provide for any kind of necessity.

From the nutritional point of view, Damanhur has an agricultural cooperative that covers a large part of the citizens' overall needs with extensive crops, vegetables, fruit orchards and cattle farming. In many communities, there are small and large gardens, food conservation projects and small animal raising—all of which make the concept of self-sufficiency even more concrete. All production is strictly organic and GMO-free.

EVERYDAY CONSIDERATIONS

At Damanhur, sustainability means being engaged on the front lines of environmental protection, economic development and social responsibility. It also means creating systems in different contexts: from management of time on a personal and collective level, to large, common investments, for example: constructing passive houses that produce all the necessary energy for everyday consumption like electricity, heating, etc. We also pay attention to changing our everyday habits, lowering environmental impact and training ourselves to conserve resources.

Damanhurian communities are built with ecological building materials, and we use renewable energy sources everyday, such as solar and photovoltaic panels, geothermal and biomass heating. We harvest seasonal organic products from the earth: vegetables, fruits, grains. We raise animals: bees, chickens, rabbits, cows, ducks, turkeys. We take care of the land, both in the fields and in the woods. We use organic septic systems, like the Imhoff system, and constructed wetland systems for grey and black water treatment. We collect rainwater and clean stream water for household use. We use organic and plant-based detergents. We compost food waste to obtain fertilizer for reuse in agriculture, and we recycle meticulously.

In short, we live in contact with nature without avoiding technology; rather, we use it in a way that is most intelligent—for humans and for the environment.

At the **Damanhur Crea** Center in Vidracco, Italy, you can find:

Tentaty, organic food store with natural products, **www.tentaty.it - tentaty@tentaty.it**

Edilarca, eco-sustainable and biocompatible construction and services,

www.edilarca.com - www.lacellulosa.com

Solerà, renewable energy, photovoltaic, solar-thermal, geothermal, biomass and wind energy systems,

www.solera.info

Solios, solutions for eco-sustainable and biocompatible construction, **www.happyandhealthyliving.it**

RESPECT FOR THE LAND

The planet is a living being to be respected and protected. To do so in the best way, from the beginning of the community, Damanhur has invested both human and financial resources to purchase and care for many hundreds of acres of agricultural and forest lands. Unfortunately, in the Upper Canavese area of Italy, many chestnut forests have been exploited for firewood, which has resulted in the loss of large fruit trees and the biodiversity that once characterized the local woods.

For nearly a decade, local chestnut trees were attacked by the gall wasp, a very aggressive parasite. To restore the woods to their original state, in addition to fighting off the gall wasp with its insect antagonist, Damanhur launched an important bioproject in 1988. We have therapeutically cut and restored the trees, and freed the forest from dead trees and plants. After an extensive effort to identify biocompatible tree and plant species for each area, we have started to reintroduce them in a way that they have ample space to grow. As a result, many species of animals have also returned to their natural habitats in these woods.

Safeguarding the water supply is also an important part of respecting and protecting our planet. In Damanhur's communities, water sources are kept clean at all times.

Rainwater is collected in storage basins and reused for crop irrigation, household use and fire fighting, if needed. Where the topography of the land has allowed for it, biotopes have been created by digging lakes and reintroducing biocompatible plant species, according to the principles of permaculture.

Bees are also present in all areas of Damanhur's communities. They serve an integral role in the natural cycle to maintain the biodiversity of plant species.

LOW-IMPACT TECHNOLOGIES

In constructing new houses, just as in renovating old ones, the objective is low environmental impact. Research and, above all, practical experience have made it possible to experiment with techniques, materials and innovative living solutions that are earth-friendly.

Green building in Damanhur begins with recuperating materials and energy conservation. We call it "bioclimatic building" because it values human beings as aware users of the space. Damanhurian architects begin with an analysis of what already exists, reusing materials as much as possible. New materials are all eco-friendly, such as clay, wood and natural lime. Many alternative solutions are intended to save energy, such as high thermal insulation and solar panel installation.

Houses that have been recently built on the grounds of Damanhur are healthy and well integrated into their natural surroundings. The older homes, renovated from farmhouses and abandoned buildings, are living a second youth.

Two Damanhur communities, Aval and Prima Stalla, have been awarded the Green Flag award by FEE Italy, an international foundation based in Denmark that promotes ecological and sustainable initiatives.

To visit Aval and Prima Stalla, in addition to all the other places in Damanhur, you may contact **Damanhur Welcome & University**, at Damjl. www.damanhur.org - Tel. +39 0124 512226.

"OLIO CALDO"

Olio Caldo is an experiment in self-sufficiency. In 1985, all citizens of Damanhur took turns experiencing a period in which we ate only self-produced food and wore only clothes and footwear that were made within the community. There was a Damanhurian house that was dedicated to this project. It was in an isolated area, with respect to the other houses, and citizens each spent about one or two weeks living there—some stayed for a few months—immersed in this dimension of complete self-sufficiency.

The means of transportation was limited to two old bicycles and a rickety hand-pulled wagon. For most of us, this experimentation period was short yet intense.

We milked a cow at six in the morning in order to have milk for breakfast. We washed our clothes by hand with ash. We made clothing from fabrics that were woven on a loom, then hand-sewn. We walked in homemade wooden shoes for miles and harvested cane to weave baskets for transporting chestnuts and other items foraged from the land. We churned cream skimmed from the milk to make butter.

We pedaled to produce the electricity needed to light the only light bulb in the house. We ate wild herbs and seasonal fruits that we harvested as our main meal, and much more.

Needless to say, this was an adventure that changed the perspectives of everyone who experienced it!

Today, "Olio Caldo 4" is the current development of the same original concept of achieving self-sufficiency, which expands the criteria for evaluating quality of life to both material and spiritual aspects. The actual dimensions of the project are no longer those of the mountain cabin thirty years ago. Since 1985, Damanhur has purchased many agricultural properties, renovated a farm where we produce organic vegetables and grains, built greenhouses throughout the communities and much more. Thirty years later, the pioneering spirit that characterized "Olio Caldo 1" is alive and always creating something new.

HEALTHY NUTRITION

The Damanhurian diet is selective about the quality of foods eaten, not about the types of food. In Damanhurian communities, an omnivorous diet is favored, one that includes meat and animal products, which are consumed with moderation and respect. Nourishment is one way to assume the experiences of the animals that one nourishes oneself with, so a diet with variety, beyond being healthy, makes it possible for more complete nourishment from a spiritual point of view. There are also citizens at Damanhur who prefer a vegetarian, vegan or raw vegan diet as a personal choice.

The quality of the food is what characterizes all the different nutritional choices. All forms of agriculture, animal raising and food conservation are carried out according to organic criteria, avoiding any risk of GMO contamination. These days, perhaps the only guarantee of food authenticity comes from knowing where and how it was produced..

Damanhurians have created a large agricultural cooperative, Punto Verde, which is responsible for extensive crops, horticulture and livestock on behalf of the entire community. Smaller initiatives also exist in the various communities: orchards, vegetable gardens, vineyards and beehives, as well as raising pigs, chickens, fish and so on. Other agricultural activities also take place in Tuscany, where many non-resident citizens of Damanhur live.

Some produce their own organic and biodynamic wines, others caretake an olive grove that is owned by Damanhur. In general, Damanhur produces grains, vegetables, fruits, milk, eggs, different kinds of meat, cheese, olive oil, baked goods, wine and honey.

You can enjoy organic meals at:

- **Arielvo** organic cafe-restaurant at Damanhur Crea in Vidracco - Tel. **+39 0125 789921**
- **Somachandra** organic cafe-restaurant at Damjl in Baldissero Canavese - **somachandrasnc@damanhur.it Tel. +39 329 1725209**
- **Il Tarassaco** organic agritourism restaurant in Cuceglio **agriturismoiltarassaco@gmail.com** Tel. **+39 328 6489398** **www.facebook.com/AgriturismoilTarassaco**
- **Principe d'Oro** restaurant in Vidracco **www.principedoro.com - Tel. +39 0125 791125 prenota@principedoro.com**

DAMANHUR CREA

Damanhur Crea is a multipurpose space that is open to the public, a "living laboratory" where ideas and dreams are translated into art objects, cultural events and eco-sustainable projects. It is an example of Damanhurian sustainability: 4,000 square meters of space shared by art studios, businesses, services, non-profit organizations, and common meeting areas. Crea is located in a former Olivetti factory, acquired by Damanhur and reopened in 2004.

The structure was built thanks to the drive of the industrialist and social reformer Adriano Olivetti, who created the complex in the 1950s to counter the growing depopulation of the valley by giving local residents a chance to work in the area.

The new use of this building is an example of recovering an abandoned industrial site.

The building was adapted to meet the needs of the businesses and services that now utilize it.

At the same time, the design respects the characteristics desired by Olivetti, according to his conception of the harmonious relationship between the individual, the work environment and the wider social context.

For Damanhurians, Damanhur Crea is not only a place where they go to work. It is also a container of diverse aspects of life, shared with visitors, friends and clients.

DAMANHUR crea

These aspects include: health and wellness, fine arts and crafts, culture and performances.

Damanhur Crea is a community of businesses—although each one is autonomous and independent from an administrative, legal and economic perspective—together they have the goal of recognizing the spiritual value in work, using it as an opportunity to change themselves and the world.

Damanhur Crea is a large laboratory where people encounter each other and exchange ideas, developing and promoting services that are characterized by the added value of this process.

Damanhur Crea is home to several businesses related to food service and nutrition, green building design and construction, a health clinic, several wellness services, art studios and non-profit organizations. The full listing of businesses, organizations and activities in Damanhur Crea is found at the back of this book, along with activities taking places in other areas of Damanhur. Damanhur Crea also houses the **"Adriano Olivetti" Conference Center**, a luminous, welcoming multi-purpose space which is suitable for hosting events and conferences of all kinds.

The Conference Center has 200 seats, video cameras and a large screen for live recordings and projections, a system for simultaneous translation in multiple languages, and live broadcast on the internet. It is the most modern structure for meetings and conferences in the Valchiusella area, and it also serves as a modern performance hall for music, dance and theatre performances. The staff of the Conference Center offers translators, multi-language hosts, and audio-video technicians for any kind of event.

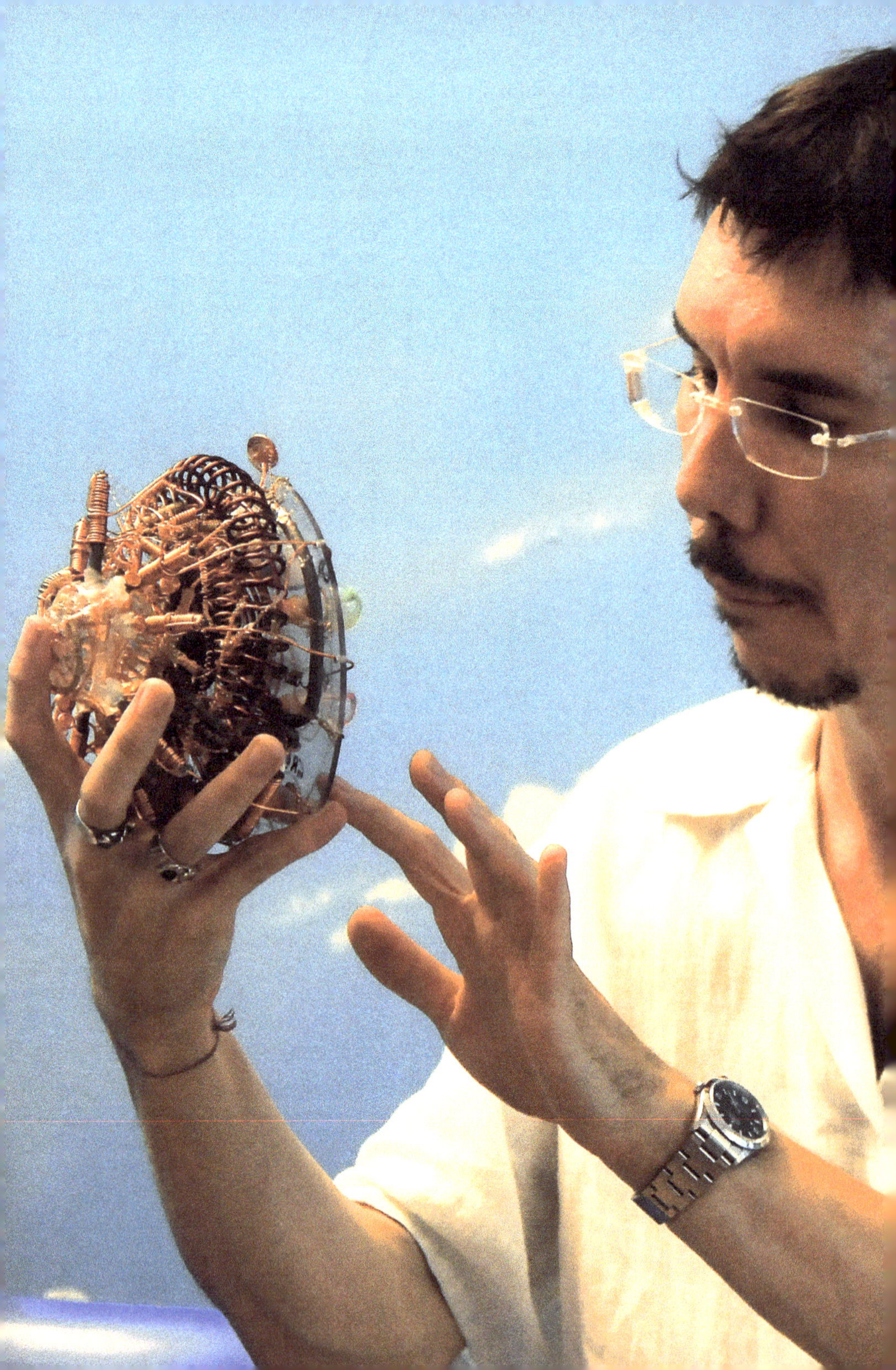

RESEARCH AND EXPERIMENTATION

EXPLORATION OF NEW PATHWAYS

At Damanhur, we consider ourselves to be a Popolo of artists and researchers in a broad sense, which extends to every aspect of existence because life is a field of continuous exploration. In Damanhur, elevating the spirit does not mean distancing ourselves from matter, but rather making every form "divine." To do so, we need to give meaning to every action completed and every object produced, adding value to each expression.

So, research and experimentation is a way of life. The goal is not only in the final results but in the process of exploring new paths. It also means trying new ways to do what you already know and opening roads that are off the beaten track in all areas: spiritual, social, cultural, healing, self-awareness, in connection with every aspect of life.

All acquired knowledge becomes a foundation for future expansion, constantly expanding horizons and going beyond the notion of stopping at a certain destination.

So, research may be expressed as a way of life and as a continual expansion of experience. In this way, its intrinsic value is increased far beyond being just a method of operation or a simple tool to obtain a result.

HEALTH AND MEDICINE

Health is not the absence of illness but the fullness of living. Good health is about having a balanced lifestyle that nourishes the body through nutrition and hygiene, as well as the mind and spirit through social relations, creative pursuits and the capacity to get out of our routines and be adaptable to any situation. Prevention plays a key role. It is important to take care of ourselves, not just when we feel ill but also when we are well. Disease is an important source of change that intervenes for different reasons in each of our lives. It is an opportunity to have a significant experience; it can be a Grail that pours profound life lessons into us.

Another fundamental illness-wellness concept is that of personal responsibility. Each of us is the creator of our own health and pathway to healing. The therapist, healer, doctor, even the surgeon, when necessary, can offer crucial help, but real healing takes place when we become accountable for ourselves.

INTEGRATIVE MEDICINE

Damanhurian medicine is preventive and syncretistic. It utilizes a number of techniques that are appropriate for the individual, and that take into consideration not just the type of pathology but the person's whole lifestyle.

This model of health begins with home birth, moves through nutrition and concludes with preparations for a good death. It uses pranatherapy as a foundation and there are also regular health screenings. Methodologies range from herbal medicine to emergency medicine, from Selfica to genetic screening: these are just some of the elements that contribute to restoring and maintaining optimal health.

At Damanhur, there are doctors, spiritual healers and holistic researchers who are available by appointment for anyone who wishes to consult with them. The Damanhurian doctors work in the Center for Integrative Medicine "Crea Salute" and FisioCrea at Damanhur Crea.

You may find the **Crea Salute** health clinic at the Damanhur Crea center, in Vidracco, Italy.
www.creasalute.it - Tel. +39 0125 789966
info@creasalute.it

DAMANHURIAN MEDICINE

Through 40 years of constantly evolving work, researchers at Damanhur have identified many healing techniques. The first level of intervention in wellness and healing are: pranatherapy and breathing, hypnosis and relaxation techniques, massage and self-massage, sound-color healing (exposure to colored lights that are associated with sound), and the use of Selfica (a discipline that creates structures with metals, liquids and prepared inks using the spiral as the basic form), which facilitates protection and recuperation of many vital functions.

The development of Selfica research in the field of wellness is one of the most important pursuits at Damanhur. In this field, experiments are conducted with verified results from many medical doctors. The Crea & Ricerca Foundation has developed a scientific protocol to verify the effectiveness of Selfica intervention on cellular well-being.

Damanhur's historical field of healing research is pranatherapy, now called "PranaPractice" as well. This technique uses radiant energy that emanates from a healer through the positioning of the hands. The healer does not transmit his or her own energy, but rather connects the client to "bioenergy," or the vital energy of the planet, which is in contact with the entire universe.

It is a simple treatment, as ancient as humankind, that supports the maintenance of good health.

Falco Tarassaco discovered that he was a natural healer when he was a teenager. Over the years, through his Airaudi School of Pranatherapy, he had refined a method for training other healers. Today, Damanhur Welcome & University organizes the School for Spiritual Healers, a three-year program of training and spiritual growth, with an option of two additional years of specialized training.

At the **Damanhur Crea** center in Vidracco, Italy, you may find Damanhurian doctors at the **Crea Salute** health clinic, the **FisioCrea** physical therapy studio, **Kythera** spa and wellness center, as well as PranaPractice treatments.

SELFICA

Selfica is a field of research that was introduced to Damanhur through Falco Tarassaco's studies and experiments, which he conducted with others in the community. The Selfica discipline makes it possible to focus and direct vital and intelligent energies to perform different functions connected to wellness, amplifying perceptions and personal development.

The structures of Selfica are based on the spiral, and they are comprised of metals, minerals, colors and special inks, all of which act as conductors for intelligent energies. These "border forces" can be a link between our material world and different planes of existence, enabling us to establish a synergistic relationship among all of them. Selfica is an ancient technology.

Building a Selfic structure is much like providing a "body" for use by the Self. The intelligence of the Self is the particular energy that manages the physical part of the structure. The interaction between the Selfs and individuals is always based on exchange: the Selfs select conditions that are useful for physical life or for the development of personal human potential. They connect to our energy fields through the "microlines," or energy lines in the body. The Self's intelligent energy selects, harmonizes and amplifies the most useful energy frequencies to perform the function for which it was built.

In exchange, the Selfica intelligence goes through an interesting experience given that they can participate in a sector of space-time that is characterized by a different relationship of laws from that of their place of origin.

Another area of Damanhur research connected to Selfica is "Selfic painting." With this art technique, intelligent energies are conveyed through two-dimensional shapes based on symbols and colors. Metals are often used in "classic" Selfica; they are translated into color, and their usual three dimensions are reduced to two in the process.

An exhibition of Selfic paintings is on permanent display at the Niatel Art Gallery in Damanhur Crea. The paintings project signals and information into the environment and toward the observers. The key to interpreting these paintings lies in precise combination of the form and its title. Each title enriches the image with the poetry that profoundly touches the heart, mind and soul.

For those who would like to experience a "Self"...

... you can go to the **ELASEL** studio on the lower level of Damanhur Crea for some of the various wellness treatments available;

... to amplify perceptions and for a meditative experience, we suggest that you go to the **NIATEL** gallery, the permanent exhibition of Selfic Paintings, and ask to be guided by the staff.
(**www.quadriselfici.it**);

... for aesthetic treatments, you can go to the **KYTHERA** studio, the only spa in the world that

prepares cosmetic products with the potential that Selfica can offer, with the use of unique instruments specially designed for beauty and wellness;
... for wellness treatments, you can see our **HOLISTIC HEALERS** such as **Cavalluccio marino Arnica**, **Tucano** and **Calabrone Farro** on the lower level of Damanhur Crea;
... to receive a Pranoself treatment, which is an application of pranatherapy amplified by Selfic structures, you can go to the **Pranoself studio** at Damjl in Baldissero Canavese.

For those who would like to purchase a "Self"...
... you can go to the **SELET** studio on the lower level of Damanhur Crea, where many Damanhurian Selfs are created (**www.sel-et.com**).

For those who want to purchase "Selfic jewelry"...
... you can go to the **OROCREA** jewelry studio on the upper level of Damanhur Crea, where Selfic art becomes jewelry (**www.orocrea.com**).

For those who want to know more about the art of Selfica...
... you can purchase the book ***Spirals of Energy*** at **Niatel** in Damanhur Crea.
... you can contact **Welcome & University** at **Damjl** for many other possibilities.

SYNCHRONIC LINES

The reason Damanhur was built in the Alto Canavese area of Italy is the simultaneous presence of four Synchronic Lines, which cross forming a junction of particular intensity in this area.

According to the teachings of Falco Tarassaco, the founder of Damanhur, the Synchronic Lines are a communication system that connects all the celestial bodies where life is found.

There are 18 main Synchronic Lines on Earth, connected to each other through minor lines. The 18 main lines are united at the north and south poles to form a single line at each pole, which project outward into the universe.

Through the Synchronic Lines, everything which is not conveyed by a physical body may travel along the whole universe... thoughts, energies, emotions, soul structures that encounter a body for a new incarnation, soul structures that journey toward new experiences after the death of the physical body, and so on. The system of Synchronic Lines is like a nervous system of the universe and of every single world. Being in contact with the Synchronic Lines means being at the center of a flow of thoughts and information that can be very inspiring, and it is possible to contribute to this flow through one's awareness and capacity to direct thought.

To know more, you may purchase the book *Synchronic Lines* at **Damanhur Crea** and at **Damanhur Welcome & University**.

THE PLANT WORLD

Damanhurians have always been active in researching communication with the forces of nature, guided by the desire to re-establish a harmonious balance in the relationship with life on our beautiful planet. In the Damanhurian Spiritual Vision, humans are part of a spiritual ecosystem with forces and intelligences, and it is important to establish a conscious contact with them, just as it is with life forms present in the environmental ecosystem that surrounds us. Our human evolution is inextricably linked to the alliance with and reunification of the physical and subtle forces that inhabit this and other worlds, which Damanhurians call the "Mother Worlds."

Plants and nature spirits are the beings that inhabit these worlds, and a large part of the research in Damanhur is dedicated to opening roads of deep contact with the "dimension" of plants and nature spirits.

SACRED WOODS TEMPLE

An example of research in this contact is the Sacred Woods Temple. Damanhur has always invested in acquiring numerous acres of woodlands that were often cut down by previous owners to have wood for heating, suffering decades of intensive exploitation.

In Damanhur's philosophy, a forest is a magical place where the complexity of life is expressed in a harmonious interweaving of many forms of animal, plant and subtle life. In Falco Tarassaco's teachings, our plane of existence is divided into a number of mother-worlds, including the world of human beings, that of nature spirits and the world of plants.

The Sacred Woods Temple now has dedicated spaces for meditation and contact with trees and nature spirits, with the intention of bringing the Mother Worlds closer together. There are also intentionally placed spirals and labyrinths that form pathways amongst and around the trees. They stretch for miles into the woods and each has a different function. They are connected to the node of Synchronic Lines that wrap around the Temples of Humankind.

Much research and many experiences have made the Sacred Woods Temple alive and full of history, like when citizens of Damanhur went to the woods together for experiments in wilderness survival, which also stimulated individual transformation for everyone.

You may request to visit the **Sacred Woods Temple**, walk the Labyrinths and spend a day visiting the woods, by contacting **Damanhur Welcome & University** at Damjl, in Baldissero Canavese, Italy, where you can also receive information about Tree Orientation.

www.damanhur.org - Tel. +39 0124 512226.

TREE ORIENTATION

Tree Orientation is an initiative that not only Damanhurians participate in, but also many friends in every part of the world, and the purpose is to bring the human and plant worlds closer together, as they once were.

The trees are large, living antennas of our planet. On the Summer Solstice, the trees launch a signal into the cosmos about the health of our planet, and at the Winter Solstice, they receive a return signal. For many years, their message has been a cry of despair because humans are destroying nature. The community of Damanhur and the many supporters of this initiative around the globe have made a commitment to transform the cries of the trees into songs of joy.

Tree Orientation is a huge endeavor, but a tremendously fun adventure. It is a project that anyone can join in by using a simple technique, which involves getting close to a tree while carrying some Selfic structures, and walking around the tree as if you were embracing it.

For information on Tree Orientation, you can go to the website **www.globaltreenetwork.com**

You can listen to the **Music of the Plants** at **Damanhur Crea** at the reception by the entrance and by **Solerà** on the lower level. Also, at **Damjl** in Baldissero Canavese at **Welcome & University**, as well as the Sacred Woods Temple and in other locations and concert settings. For information, contact **Damanhur Welcome & University** **www.damanhur.org - Tel. +39 0124 512226.**

You may purchase a Music of the Plants device at

- **Solerà** at Damanhur Crea
- **Damanhur Welcome & University** at Damjl
- at **www.musicoftheplants.com**

MUSIC OF THE PLANTS

The Music of the Plants research began in Damanhur in 1976, when resident researchers created an instrument that was able to capture the electromagnetic variations of the surface of plant leaves and roots and turn them into sounds.

The desire for deep contact with nature has also inspired the "Plant Concerts," in which musicians perform while accompanied by melodies created by trees. The trees learn to control their electrical emissions, so they can modulate the notes, as if they are aware of the music they are producing. This research has continued, and today, the device used for concerts is available to the general public so that this profound experience of plant world communication may be shared by anyone who wishes to do so.

Music of the Plants concerts are held regularly at Damanhur. They have also been presented at festivals in Europe, India, the United States and Canada. Many of these experiences have been recorded and arranged into music collections and CDs.

You can buy the book ***Music of the Plants*** and **CDs** at **Tentaty** in Damanhur Crea and at **Welcome & University** at Damjl.

A SHARED CULTURE

A LONG STORY

At the base of every choice in Damanhur are philosophical and spiritual motivations. The dream of creating a sustainable society originated with the idea that life in all its manifestations is an expression of the same divine energy. We believe that we should do our best to awaken awareness of how we are deeply united with every element of life that surrounds us. This heartfelt belief has motivated Damanhurians to invest not only in environmental, social and economic sustainability, but also cultural sustainability.

Damanhurians have created myths, stories, plays and other forms of expression to create union among people and encourage the sharing of values and principles. For this reason, Damanhur itself is sort of like an epic novel shared through different ways of expression, so adults and children, Damanhur citizens and friends all take turns sharing our stories and listening to each other.

The concept of creating an original culture may not seem as concrete an application of sustainability as something like, for instance, growing organic food, but at

Damanhur, we strive to make "every action poetic" and "every poetry concrete." So, little by little, we have created original myths that were initially proposed by Falco, then developed by many Damanhurians into theatre shows, musical compositions, and other forms of expression.

The roles of the creators/producers and the audience are circular: there are those who write, those who paint, those who applaud. There are the critics, those who act out the roles, others who provide the inspiration and those who translate it. They are the same people in different roles, depending on whether we are talking about theatre, music, painting and so on.

Even the custom of decorating and painting all of the exterior walls of our buildings and houses with flowers, plants and animals, as is evident for those who visit Damjl, reminds us of the importance of the ecosystem in which we are immersed. Like all of our endeavors as a community, it is a response to the desire for a collective identity shared through the timeless simplicity of a good story.

Culture is not just for intellectuals, and art is not just for connoisseurs. Both are popular sentiments that create the plot and the threads along which ideals and shared values flow. The Temples of Humankind, where the cultural, artistic and spiritual aspects of the Damanhur experience come together, are the best representation of this vision.

A POPOLO OF ARTISTS (AND ASPIRING ONES...)

At Damanhur, everyone can dream and express their creative side by making new works of art and having new experiences. Living with an artistic spirit means adding value and meaning to everyday life, exceeding previous results by opening the gateway to higher intuition, which serves to make our lives the best masterpiece of all.

Since its beginning years, the values and meanings that characterize Damanhurian life and its philosophy have taken on a voice and form through a privileged channel of art.

Through art, Damanhurian citizens explore their creative potential—even those who have no prior art experience. In fact, many have started as self-taught artists, experimenting with even the more refined forms of art, such as marble inlay work and Tiffany stained glass. Over the years, the results that these artists achieved have rewarded the initiative with which they collectively created works that are unique in their scale and originality.

The most significant testimony to what has been achieved in this pathway of communal artistic research is the Temples of Humankind, a complex network of underground halls and corridors, dug out by hand with devotion and transformed into a treasure trove of art and meanings.

Damanhurian philosophy states that the most valuable works of art are the ones we create within ourselves through experiences that help us to become more mature, aware and creative. "Making art" is a concept that permeates every aspect of life.

Artistic experience at Damanhur is always open to friends and visitors, and many of the art installations on Damanhur's territories come from their contributions made during courses and seminars.

Each Damanhurian engages in at least one kind of art form. Year after year, a more specific style is developed by identifying shared canons, which are manifested in different forms of expressive and figurative art. Today, from the paintings of the Temple halls to theatrical sketches that bring lightheartedness to many public meetings, artistic expression is an element present in the life of every Damanhurian, where everyone is both artist and audience.

The artist is seen as a medium of the people. A painter, a writer, a sculptor is someone who knows how to channel the inspiration that comes from all Damanhurians—volunteering one's own hands, ingenuity and voice to the collective creation. For this reason, artwork that is created is a piece of a common identity, in which every Damanhurian recognizes a part of themselves in it.

You may find works of **Damanhurian artists** in the art studios of the **Damanhur Crea center**, in Vidracco, Italy.

THE TEMPLES OF HUMANKIND

Damanhur is visited every year by thousands of people, attracted by its history and programs for renewal and study. However, most visitors come to see the Temples of Humankind, a great underground construction excavated by hand out of the rock of a mountain by Damanhur citizens. It is a sacred work of art, unique in the world, dedicated to the divine nature of every human being. In this work of art, thanks to the devotion of Damanhurians, the love for life and beauty characterize every mosaic square, every brushstroke of color, every piece of glass. They create a bridge between our ancient past and the present, sketching a future of spiritual harmony between human beings and Gods.

The Temples are a large three-dimensional book that narrates the history of humankind, through all forms of art. They are a pathway of reawakening the divine within and beyond the self. Here, every detail has a meaning: the colors, the measurements, every detail follows a precise code of forms and proportions. Every hall has its own specific "frequency" and voice, made audible in many ways, including the musical instruments inside it.

The Temples of Humankind symbolically represent the inner rooms of every human being. Walking through the halls and corridors corresponds to a profound journey within oneself.

The Temples are over 8,500 cubic meters on five different levels, connected by hundreds of meters of hallways. They are connected to the four Synchronic Lines that flow through this area, creating a "shining node," that is, a point where the Lines encounter each other and form a kind of large antenna for receiving messages, intuitions and information about the planet and the whole universe.

For Damanhurians, the halls of this great underground work of art are laboratories where art and science, technology and spirituality come together in seeking new roads for the evolution of humankind. Just as it was in the medieval and the Renaissance with the construction of large cathedrals, building the Temples of Humankind has created the opportunity for realizing arts and crafts studios, which Damanhur is appreciated for all over the world.

The citizens of Damanhur hold celebrations and encounters in the Temples connected to each person's spiritual path, and everyone contributes to the maintenance and development of the works within the Temples. The Temples of Humankind are open to visits every day, and their halls can host visits and meditations based on the requests of individuals and groups.

You may request to visit the **Temples of Humankind** at the **Damanhur Welcome & University**, at Damjl, in Baldissero Canavese, Italy. **www.damanhur.org Tel. + 39 0124 512226.** For more information about the **Temples of Humankind** visit **www.thetemples.org**

SPIRITUAL VISION

A PHILOSOPHY OF LIFE

Damanhur was born and has been developed as a spiritual experience.

Inspired by its founder Falco Tarassaco, Damanhur's philosophy is based on positive thinking, action, and the idea that every individual desires to leave something of themselves to others and contribute to the evolution of humanity.

In the Damanhurian vision of spirituality, we are all part of a spiritual ecosystem that is comprised of diverse conscious beings, and it is important to be aware of them and establish contact. In this ecosystem, there are beings whom humanity has always contacted in different ways, from the nature spirits that live in the woods to the divinities present in the pantheons of many Popoli.

Humans share in this ecosystem because we each carry a divine spark. The goal of the Damanhurian spiritual path is to reawaken this divine spark, which corresponds to the ultimate potential within, in each of us.

Living with this divine principle means acknowledging that spirituality permeates every moment of existence, 24 hours a day, from birth to death.

In Damanhur, the highest vision of the relationship between human and divine is represented by the "Triad." In the Triad, the divinities of all peoples of the planet, which have often been separated and in conflict, are connected in complete harmony. Those with similar myths and characteristics are united with each other, to create and strengthen a new global alliance between humanity and the divine, able to reawaken consciousness and a sense of unity—rather than separation—in all of humanity.

SECULAR SPIRITUALITY

Damanhur offers a practical philosophy of life in which spirituality gives meaning to and recognizes the significance in every aspect of life.

Damanhur is neither a cult nor a religion, as it does not offer a revealed truth to follow. Instead, the secular message of Damanhur invites everyone to seek answers to life's fundamental questions within themselves, but through exchange and discussion with others.

The Damanhurian philosophy puts human beings and gods on the same evolutionary path: the gods have different characteristics, although, like us, they are part of the very nature of the universe. The gods are part of the same ecosystem in which every intelligent being, human, spirit and divinity, realizes their evolution in relation to the evolution of others.

The belief that humanity has a divine origin influences our relationship with divinities. For Damanhurians, in a secular sense, this partnership is based on respect and exchange. Rituals are the language through which we communicate with divine forces, and not an act of submission or devotion in and of itself. In fact, the main objective of the initiation that takes place in the School of Meditation is to establish an alliance between humans and gods in order to support both on our evolutionary paths.

The reawakening of each person's divine spark can occur through spiritual paths that are very different from one another because at the center of spiritual exploration, we are individuals with great diversity. Damanhurians view this diversity as true wealth that we have at our disposal. Ultimately, growing, evolving and improving as human beings means one thing: continuously expanding our capacity of knowledge and empathy for life that surrounds us, in all its forms.

Damanhur's spiritual message is accessible to anyone who wishes to explore it more deeply. From the outset, Falco Tarassaco, founder and spiritual guide of Damanhur, has made his teachings available in courses and seminars, as well as through various writings and publications.

THE QUESITI

The "Quesiti" are dynamic formulas, themes that can be used for meditation and also applied in everyday life. Their formulation is the result of the collective achievements of Damanhur, but each person can interpret them according to their own talents and characteristics.

The **First** Quesito emphasizes the importance of action and choice, to live life fully and with purity of intentions.

The **Second** Quesito calls for constancy and continuity, to give meaning and importance to choices that have been made, and it emphasizes the importance of keeping one's word.

The **Third** Quesito calls for a change in logic to welcome new visions of self, of life and of the sacred dimension of existence. This is the first step in creating a civilization and culture.

The **Fourth** Quesito, specifically feminine, encourages men and women to discover their feminine side, openness and availability, and the profound awareness of representing a stable element of union.

The **Fifth** Quesito brings attention to the masculine energies present in each one of us, to the capacity to live in constant and harmonious inner revolution.

The **Sixth** Quesito invites us to unite the masculine and feminine principles within ourselves, to activate our power of creation, not only of life itself, but also of its representations through art and creativity, generosity and kindness.

The **Seventh** Quesito calls for the use of the doubt and adaptability as research tools to abandon all dogmas and certainties, to discover what is true inside of us, beyond appearances.

Finally, the **Eighth** Quesito invites projecting our attention towards others. It speaks of Love and teaching as instruments to transform the world around us; study as spiritual necessity; the irreversible choice of our own ideals, to achieve the reawakening of our divine principle and be "in the service to the world."

SPIRITUAL PHYSICS

According to Damanhur philosophy, alongside the laws of physics and chemistry are the laws of a parallel science that explain the emergence of forms and life derived from the spiritual energies that pervade the universe. Spiritual Physics, also called Esoteric Physics, comes from the research and explorations of this vast field, according to the teachings of Falco Tarassaco, the founder of Damanhur. On a spiritual path, research that leads "outside" ourselves is always a road that leads to new discoveries "within" ourselves as well. In this light, the investigation of reality conducted from the perspective of Spiritual Physics is complementary to that of the School of Meditation, because they share the same goals.

Damanhur Welcome & University regularly organizes Spiritual Physics seminars and courses for anyone who wishes to explore these topics.

You may ask for information about courses on **Spiritual Physics** at **Damanhur Welcome & University**, at Damjl, in Baldissero Canavese, Italy. **www.damanhur.org - Tel. +39 0124 512226**. You may further explore the subject with the book *Spiritual Physics*.

SCHOOL OF MEDITATION

The School of Meditation is a spiritual research pathway based on sharing and self-transformation, with the intention to awaken the divine within each human being through the creative power of positive thinking. In its 40-year history, the School has stimulated and enriched the lives of Communities within Damanhur, and has welcomed spiritual seekers from all over the world.

The School of Meditation involves the activation of a direct relationship with the forces of the spiritual ecosystem, through an initiation. There is no charge to enroll, as the knowledge that is accessed cannot be priced.

In the first meetings, the meaning of life is explored, as well as the laws and forces that govern the universe. The research then takes on a chosen direction through Spiritual Ways—six specific pathways to express spirituality in practice, according to one's personal characteristics and preferences. At a certain level, exploring the various themes of Meditation is determined by the members of the School.

In the Damanhurian vision, an authentic spiritual path leads to the awakening of the master within each one of us, through a process of refining one's perceptions and transforming one's limitations, which happens when one is open to the help that we can give to and receive from others.

The School of Meditation teaches us to not delegate our personal spiritual evolution to someone outside of ourselves.

This is why Meditation is seen as a way of daily life, a pathway in which the School can last a lifetime if one so desires.

The School of Meditation also offers Path to Spiritual Freedom, which deepens an exploration of Falco Tarassaco's teachings. The path involves a series of reflections and experiences that support each individual in their personal spiritual experience, including those that are not directly connected to Damanhur, and in seeking their mission in life.

For information about the **School of Meditation**, write to: **damanhurmeditazione@damanhur.it**

FALCO TARASSACO, THE FOUNDER OF DAMANHUR

Damanhur was founded by Falco Tarassaco, Oberto Airaudi, whom Damanhurians consider to be their spiritual guide.

Falco was a man who strongly believed in his own dreams, so much so that he was able to involve others, opening up a chance for them to dream as well. He departed from his physical body in June of 2013.

In 1975, when he was already well known as a pranatherapy practitioner, a medium and para-psychologist, Falco, together with some of his friends, created the basis for what would become Damanhur.

He felt he had an important mission: to create a spiritual society founded on research and action, where women and men together can experience a new equilibrium between human beings, divine forces and natural forces. To do this, he dedicated himself to studying human potential, the profound energies of nature, the magical and esoteric traditions, proposing new and original experiences, like the study of spirals and their energies (Selfica), a very particular kind of visionary painting, and a reinterpretation of classical myths in a key that puts human beings at the center of the relationship between nature, humankind and divine forces.

Falco was a tireless researcher in different fields, and he maintained an intense dialog with Damanhurians about this research during Thursday evening meetings, which he conducted uninterrupted from 1988 until just a few days before his death.

Falco's charisma was that of a man who was strongly convinced of his own mission and therefore capable of dedicating exceptional energy to it, with great coherence. Beyond his smile, quick and ready intelligence, and inexhaustible ideas, he was striking in his ability to always stay concentrated on the objective of Damanhur, which he dedicated all his attention to.

This absolute dedication often created a resonance with those who contacted him.

His vitality and desire to act, to create a new world, beginning with Damanhur, was inevitably contagious.

For Damanhurians, Falco was and is a spiritual guide, a human being gifted with the capacity to enter into contact with the great reservoirs of universal knowledge, to extract useful information and to give rise to new sciences and spiritual paradigms, like Spiritual Physics, the pathway of the Quesiti, his vision of the spiritual ecosystem, rituals and initiation, all contained in the Damanhur School of Meditation, the heart of his teachings.

In Damanhur, there are two particular places where Damanhurians and visitors may have direct contact with the works of Falco Tarassaco. The first is the Niatel gallery of Selfic paintings in Damanhur Crea, where there is an exhibition of Falco's canvases and those of his students, who continue the tradition of Selfic painting. The second is the "Falco Tarassaco—Oberto Airaudi" Museum, at the Aval community, dedicated to his life and teachings.

You may find Falco Tarassaco's **Selfic paintings** at the **Niatel** Gallery in the Damanhur Crea center in Vidracco, Italy. **www.quadriselfici.it**
You may also find his books at **Tentaty** and in the **Niatel** Gallery at the Damanhur Crea center in Vidracco, Italy and at **Damanhur Welcome & University**, at Damjl, in Baldissero Canavese, Italy.

THE "POPOLO SPIRITUALE"

The desire to recognize ourselves as part of a common soul has inspired those at Damanhur to conceive of the idea of creating a new Popolo made up of different ethnicities and cultures, strongly united around shared values. The Popolo Spirituale is an extension of the concept of the Damanhurian Popolo, and participation is open to anyone who wishes to contribute—according to their own beliefs—to the spiritual and material growth of the planet through solidarity, mutual respect and love for the environment.

Today, people from all over the world who practice diverse philosophies and beliefs are part of the Popolo Spirituale. What we have in common is the desire to grow, respect all beings and cultures, and seek new questions and new answers. The Popolo is a container of ideals for each one of us—on our own secular, spiritual, religious pathways—to feel united with others, as one.

The Popolo Spirituale is a collective entity, alive and in constant evolution, which arises from the integration of the characteristics, experiences and aspirations of all those who choose to join. It energetically connects its members, contains their experiences and allows them to be shared amongst all who take part.

In Damanhur's philosophy, a super-entity of this kind has a much more extensive intelligence and resources than what would result from the sum of its individual members. We can compare the Popolo to a human body where everyone is a cell, and through interaction with other cells, it develops functions that would otherwise be unthinkable. To express this concept, referring to the Communities of the Federation and the research groups that citizens participate in, Damanhurians use the term "superindividual," which emphasizes how each person contributes to creating and identifying with a large collective individual.

Being a Popolo means sharing ideals, culture, art, and creating a model of life in accordance with our principles. We value diversity and integrate it into a common dream: the reawakening of humanity. The Popolo Spirituale is a reservoir of spiritual strength, and those who choose to join can receive energy and inspiration from it.

For information and to enter into the **Popolo Spirituale** of Damanhur write to:
popolo@damanhur.it

HOW TO PARTICIPATE

Becoming part of the Popolo Spirituale is very simple: emailing **popolo@damanhur.it** will make it possible to establish a first contact and receive more detailed information. At some point, it is important to come and visit us at Damanhur. Participation in the Popolo does not depend on being a citizen and living in the community, yet it is important to directly know the place where it all originates, and for us to get to know you!

A simple and intimate entrance ceremony creates the connection with the Popolo. During this ceremony, which takes less than half an hour, you will receive a bracelet that keeps you in contact—both symbolically and energetically—with the entire Popolo.

The members of the Popolo are also connected in a practical way through an exchange network that keeps everyone updated on news of the Popolo and its members. In this way, we help each other out with a sense of mutual support and caring. Those who are part of the Popolo Spirituale think positively and optimistically, giving energy to events that are positive for the future of the planet and its inhabitants, both as individuals and in groups.

DAMANHUR
HRVATSKA
most

Templi dell'Umanità
DAMANHUR
I Templi dell'Umanità
DAMANHUR
The Temples of Humankin
Nascosta nel cuore di una montagna, a nord di Torino, c'è una costruzione magica, una moderna cattedrale che molti hanno definito "l'Ottava Meraviglia del Mondo".
I Templi possono essere visitati tutti i giorni, utilizzati per la meditazione individuale o di gruppo, e per celebrare i momenti più importanti della vita. Ogni Scuola spirituale è benvenuta e può utilizzare le Sale per le sue cerimonie.

DAMANHUR IN THE WORLD

OFFERING EXPERIENCE

Damanhur is inspired to spread its spiritual message throughout the world in order to reawaken individual potential through community living, love and respect for life, solidarity and practical idealism.

Every day, Damanhurians demonstrate their commitment toward a better world, with the hope of inspiring others to do the same by encouraging those who are committed to changing their own future and the future of the planet.

Damanhur offers 40 of experience for supporting the growth of new intentional communities. There is no interest in proselytizing.

Damanhurians are engaged in promoting an innovative vision of how humanity can live together through the creation of diverse communities and valuing the identity of diverse cultures. For this reason, the Damanhurian concept of "community" is that of a large social and spiritual being who keeps up an intense dialog with the world, from the surrounding area to the most distant countries, to offer one's vision of life and of the future.

AMBASSADORS

Ambassadors are "Damanhurians with a suitcase." They travel around the world to share the experiences of Damanhur and the teachings of Falco Tarassaco.

In many countries, they have established relationships with other holistic organizations that regularly host conferences, courses and activities related to Damanhur. Each ambassador concentrates on a specific geographic location, where they periodically visit, creating a network of friends and connections.

Ambassadors carry out activities such as the courses of the School of Meditation, the Path to Spiritual Freedom, Tree Orientation, and updates on events at Damanhur, as well as Damanhur Welcome & University courses.

Ambassadors are currently working in Croatia, Germany, Japan, Denmark, Norway, the Netherlands, Spain, United States, Canada and Switzerland.

One of their objectives is to assist in creating Damanhur Centers where other Damanhurians contribute as well, and there are events and activities to offer a more complete experience and teaching in all fields.

For information, please contact the various locations listed at: **www.damanhur.org/en/share-experiences/damanhur-in-the-world**

DAMANHUR **CENTERS**

DAMANHUR CENTERS

Damanhur Centers are places of activity, research and the dissemination of information related to Damanhur. They are places where courses, seminars, School of Meditation groups and other activities are held. The subject matter of the specific activities offered by a center depends on the characteristics of the local area, such as agriculture, arts and crafts, volunteering, and so on.

Since the opening of the first historic Damanhur Center in Turin, Italy, a common feature of all Damanhur Centers is offering studies of Pranatherapy and Holistic Medicine.

Damanhur, in fact, first developed through the structure of these Centers. In 1975, when we dreamed of creating our first community, there were already several Centers established in the main cities of Piedmont, Italy. Today, Damanhur Centers are located throughout Italy, in some European countries and even in a few far away places such as Japan.

In many cases, members of these centers are Damanhur citizens who reside abroad; they are called "non-resident citizens."

These are the active Damanhur Centers, at the beginning of the year 2015:

In Italy

Bergamo, Bologna, Firenze, Milano, Modena, Torino Verona

In the world

Kobe, Japan
Tokyo, Japan
Oosterbeek, Netherlands
Vienna, Austria
Zagreb, Croatia

In many countries, Damanhurian ambassadors have established relationships and regularly host conferences, courses and activities related to Damanhur.

For information, contact the various locations listed at: **www.damanhur.org/en/share-experiences/damanhur-in-the-world**

COMMUNITY NETWORKS

Over the years, Damanhur has promoted initiatives that weave threads among various groups that have a shared concern about the future of our world, even though they may work in diverse areas of interest.

In 1981, Damanhur organized the first conference for Italian spiritual communities, with the idea of creating a collaborative network among different groups that are united by similar goals. In the following years, networks were created to connect communities, environmental movements, and the world of spiritual and ethical research, of which Damanhur is a part.

Damanhur is currently a member of the Global Ecovillage Network (GEN, www.gen.ecovillage.org) an international non-governmental organization (NGO) that is consultative member of the Economic and Social Council (ECOSOC) of the United Nations. GEN brings the experiences of the major communities of the world together and supports the transformation of traditional rural villages into sustainable ecovillages.

Damanhur was also among the founders of **Conacreis** (National Coordination of Associations and Communities of Ethical Spiritual Research, **www.conacreis.it**) in 1998. Conacreis gathers and coordinates Italian groups connected to secular and ethical spiritual research.

It also organizes training courses about organizations, cultural and social events—and, most of all, raises public awareness about non-religious spiritual and philosophical groups.

Damanhur also takes part in the Italian Ecovillage Network (RIVE, www.ecovillaggi.it), a network of large and small communities that draw attention to environmental impact, resilience, renewable energy and ecological communication.

From the synergy between GEN, Conacreis and RIVE, a project was created for the recognition of intentional communities in Italian and European law. It has been submitted to the Italian Parliament and is in the process of being presented at the European Court of Human Rights in Strasbourg, France for approval as a European law.

WORLD INITIATIVES

As Damanhurians, we like to share our experiences in the areas of social, ecological and cultural matters, so that they can be useful to others who are working towards making the world a better place. We also want to learn from others' valuable experiences in order to continually transform ourselves and our reality.

With this intention, representatives of Damanhur have actively participated over the years (often as speakers on behalf of Damanhur or our partner organizations) at international events that are dedicated to issues related to sustainability, spiritual freedom and solidarity.

Here are just a few:

- "A Symphony of Transformation, Human Forum 2008," San José, Costa Rica, March 2008.
- "First European Human Forum, Alliance for a New Humanity," Barcelona, Spain, November 2008.
- "State of the World Forum," Belo Horizonte, Brazil, August 2009.
- "Earth Charter, Tenth Anniversary," The Hague, Netherlands, June 2010.
- "Non-Governmental Organizations Conference, United Nations Department of Public Information," Bonn, Germany, September 2011.
- "Rio+20: United Nations Conference on Sustainable Development," Rio de Janeiro, Brazil, June 2012.
- "World Parliament of Spirituality," Hyderabad, India, December 2012.
- "United Nations Climate Change Conference," Copenhagen, Denmark, December 2012.

In May 2014, Damanhur formalized a sister city relationship with the Senegalese ecovillage Guédé Chantier, which is part of a Senegal government project for the transformation of small rural villages into sustainable settlements.

... we'll stop here for now, seeing that this book's publication date is 2015!

A VISIT TO DAMANHUR

COME VISIT

Damanhurians gladly welcome visitors. There are some areas that are most recommended for a visit, as they represent the experience of Damanhur citizens in a more complete way. Among these is: Damjl—the location where the first Damanhur community was founded, Damanhur Crea, and much more.

Of course, a particularly meaningful visit is going to see the Temples of Humankind, which are the most complete expression of Damanhurian philosophy, where harmony and beauty are pathways for achieving the awareness of our own spiritual nature, together with others.

To visit Damanhur, it is necessary to make a reservation for a guided visit to the various territories. On the other hand, Damanhur Crea is open to the public every day, also on holidays.

There are many modalities for visiting Damanhur: from the Sunday afternoon visit to longer periods, staying in our guest accommodations; from study programs and courses to renewal and wellness programs, to specialized programs that can be crafted to meet your needs and desires.

The Damanhur Welcome Office and Damanhur Welcome University, who take care of all aspects of hospitality, are located at Damjl.

For information, please contact **Damanhur Welcome & University** at Damjl, in Baldissero Canavese, Italy - **www.damanhur.org**
Tel. +39 0124 512226.

NO SMOKING, PLEASE

Damanhurians do not smoke, either indoors or outdoors, and we also request that all guests do not smoke when you are at Damanhur.

The abolition of smoking, which has been chosen by Damanhurians since the founding of the community for the value of self-discipline and attention toward oneself and others, is the only prohibition set forth in the Damanhurian Constitution, which otherwise calls on the capacity for self-control and the importance of avoiding exces in any behavior.

DAMANHUR WELCOME & UNIVERSITY

Damanhur Welcome & University makes the experiences of Damanhur available through courses and extended programs called "Schools."

The activities of DWU are offered to all those who seek a pathway of growth and learning that harmoniously integrates with any kind of spiritual path. The instructors are all Damanhurians who, over the years, have explored and developed the research themes introduced by Falco Tarassaco.

The fields of exploration range over extremely diverse areas, and they all originate from the teachings of Falco Tarassaco and the experience of Damanhurians, from spiritual healing to communion with nature and its forces, from border sciences to the exploration of time and past lives, from the development of individual potential to holistic wellness. At DWU, there are five extended programs called "Schools": The School of Alchemy, the School for Spiritual Healers, the Community School, the Damanhurian Art School and the Mystery School.

You may find **Damanhur Welcome & University** at Damjl, in Baldissero Canavese, Italy under the portico. **www.damanhur.org**
Tel. +39 0124 512226.

sand gear

DAMANHUR WELCOME OFFICE

The Damanhur Welcome Office organizes visits to Damanhur lasting one or more days, with programs related to art, renewal, wellness, study and so on. Every visitor may choose the duration and characteristics of the program that correspond to their expectations for a visit to Damanhur, choosing among half-day programs, one, three, and five-day programs. For longer periods, the programs may be personalized even further. Regardless of the length of stay, a visit to Damanhur is an opportunity to relax and do some inner reflection, along with being in contact with an original and welcoming community. It is possible to organize visits to the Temples of Humankind and meditations in the halls of the Temples, with different modalities, depending on the level of deepened exploration that you desire.

At Damanhur, there are accommodations with a range of prices and characteristics, from the community guesthouse for large groups to hotels in nearby areas with agreed-upon discounts for Damanhur visitors. The objective of DWO is to make it possible for everyone to craft the modality for their own visit to Damanhur.

You may find the **Damanhur Welcome Office** at Damjl, under the portico. You can find information on all the programs described here, as well as general information. **www.damanhur.org - Tel. +39 0124 512226**.

DAMJL

DAMJL

Damjl is the first place that is usually visited. It's the first Damanhur community, inaugurated in 1979. Damjl represents the history of Damanhur, beginning with the first community house, delimited by "Piazza Horus" and "Piazza dello Studio," with external walls completely decorated with flowers, field animals, and portraits of Damanhurians who have passed on over the years, though we like to consider them as still with us.

At Damjl, there are many ceramic and young stone statues, representing divinities of diverse pantheons, and hundreds of red clay statues that visitors have made and left as a gift, to leave a mark from their stay here.

There are many stone pathways in spirals and other shapes that are the outcome of a typical area of Damanhurian research: realizing an energetic exchange with the land through the creation of pathways where energy gradually accumulates. The energy is stabilized by the presence of stones, as minerals have the capacity to "remember," that is, to stabilize an energy field. These stone paths are "natural gymnasiums" where, by walking them, people can receive a regenerative effect on their energy bodies, with stimulation for functions such as digestion, memory and sleep.

The element that most characterizes Damjl is the Open Temple, which features eighteen clay columns

and two in young stone, delimited by the altar dedicated to the Earth element and the one dedicated to the Fire element. The Open Temple—which is also architecturally open, as it is directly exposed to the sky—is dedicated to that which is considered one of the most precious aspects of human beings in Damanhurian philosophy: the "sense of the divine." The sense of the divine is the inner yearning that drives each one of us to ask ourselves: What is the real nature of life and the universe? According to Damanhurians, everyone responds to this question in the way that is best for them, by turning to a religion, embarking on a philosophical journey, seeking a spiritual experience, or by embracing a purely mechanistic vision of existence. If developed on a practical level and with consistency, all these visions have equal dignity. The important thing is the question, more than the answer.

At the far west of the Open Temple, there is the Damjl amphitheater, where one area of the rounded space has been built like an ancient theatre that hosts performances, assemblies and moments of togetherness.

At Damjl, there is also a Damanhur guesthouse and classrooms for hosting many of the Damanhur Welcome & University study programs.

DAMANHUR CREA

The Damanhur Crea center hosts many studios, stores and services that make it a fundamental part of a visit to Damanhur.

Much space is dedicated to the Niatel gallery of Selfic paintings which exhibits Falco's works and the works made by those who carry on the tradition of Selfic painting.

At Damanhur Crea, there is also a collection of Damanhurian relics and historical objects, in a kind of history museum that reveals many curious aspects of our forty years of living together. By simply exiting one storefront and entering into the next, you can: do grocery shopping, get a haircut, buy a house, indulge in a spa treatment, order a photovoltaic system for your house, and model clay to decorate a small statue, fountain or capital (if you have a column in your house that needs decorating...). And finally, of course, have lunch at the organic restaurant.

For information, contact the reception at **+39 0125 789999** or **crea@damanhur.it**

SACRED WOODS TEMPLE

Damanhurians consider the woods as a temple. In the area of the Sacred Woods Temple, there are some Damanhurian houses among the chestnut, birch and oak trees, where maximum attention is given to the necessity for silence and careful environmental impact in the woods. Throughout the woods, there are stone labyrinths and paths like those in Damjl, which meander through the clearings and over the hill slopes. Walking them has the effect of entering ever more into harmony with oneself and the energies of the land. You can also find altars, standing stones and a large circle for Solstice and Equinox rituals.

According to some, if you pay attention you may encounter some unusual creatures like gnomes and elves.

The Sacred Woods Temple was the original point of inspiration for the Tree Orientation operations that Damanhurians and friends have been conducting all over the world in recent years. It is a project that involves the entire plant world in the reunification of the Mother Worlds of our planet, which is done by putting plants "online" in every area of Earth. To date, millions of individual plants have been oriented on five continents.

Today, the Sacred Woods Temple is accessible through Damanhur Welcome & University to all guests who wish to walk the spirals and labyrinths or attend a Music of the Plants concert.

PRIMA STALLA

The Prima Stalla community is the location for Damanhur's main agricultural activity. Here you can find greenhouses for horticultural production, extensive crops, many beehives and a cattle stable.

Prima Stalla is also home to the "Tarassaco" (Dandelion) Agritourism, where products fresh from the farm and garden are prepared with original recipes. Crops, livestock, food preserves, and cooked meals are all organic and GMO-free.

These are some of the possible itineraries to visit Damanhur. There are others, based on one day or multiple day packages, which can be booked at the office of Damanhur Welcome & University.

For information about the agritourism:
agriturismoiltarassaco@gmail.com
www.facebook.com/AgriturismoilTarassaco

Since the activities of **Damanhur** and those that are useful for guests are spread out over different areas, we offer you the following list, divided by topic.
The activities written in red with the **Damanhur Crea** logo are those located at the **Damanhur Crea center** in Vidracco. The others include contact information for you to be able to reach them. For any other needs not listed here, please contact **Welcome & University.**

WHERE TO EAT AND BUY FOODS

"ARIELVO" Cafe and restaurant
Open every day - **Tel. +39 0125 789921.**

"TENTATY"organic food store and natural products
Fruits and vegetables, fresh bread, meat and salami, special dietary needs, baby foods, various certified organic foods, books, herbal medicines, cosmetics, cleaning supplies including bulk for refillable bottles. **Tel. +39 0125 789917**
www.tentaty.it - tentaty@tentaty.it

"SOMACHANDRA"
A pause for refreshment in the heart of Damanhur, with drinks, cold and hot dishes, pastries, and things too for lovers of the biological and for those with intolerances.
Via Pramarzo, 3 - Baldissero Canavese
Tel. + 39 0124 512226 - somachandrasnc@damanhur.it

"PRINCIPE D'ORO" Pizzeria Restaurant
Piazza Commendator M. Ceratto, 5 (next to the town hall), Vidracco (TO) - **www.principedoro.com**
prenota@principedoro.com - Tel. +39 0125 791125.

"IL TARASSACO" Agritourism
Meat from the farm, vegetables from our fields,
fresh homemade pasta and bread, homemade desserts.
Cascina Dezzutti - Cuceglio (TO).
www.facebook.com/AgriturismoilTarassaco
agriturismoiltarassaco@gmail.com - Tel. +39 328 6489398.

"OPERE CASEARIE" **Cheesemaker** Scarabeo Rafano
Gourmet cheeses made from mountain milk of cows, goats and sheep. Gelato making studio. Magnolia's sheep milk ice cream at Arielvo in the summer.
scarabeo@damanhur.it - Tel. +39 320 7471753.

WHERE TO STAY

At the "DAMANHUR WELCOME OFFICE" you can find information about our guest houses.
Via Pramarzo, 3 - Baldissero Canavese.
www.damanhur.org - Tel. +39 0124 512226.

"PRINCIPE D'ORO" Pizzeria Restaurant – Bed and Breakfast'
Piazza Commendator M. Ceratto, 5 (next to the town hall), Vidracco - **www.principedoro.com**
prenota@principedoro.com - Tel. +39 0125 791125.

WHERE TO FIND FINE ARTS AND CRAFTS

"ARTILE" Artistic works
Mosaics: furnishings, home decorations, and courses.
Lupa Lampone - lupalampone@libero.it
Tel. + 39 320 7471764
Glass: tiffany, glass-fusion, glass painting, hot and cold glass, art objects, courses.

Piovra Caffè - piovra@damanhur.it - Tel. + 39 348 6011670
Testuggine Cacao - testuggine@damanhur.it
Painting: trompe l'oeil, skyscapes and clouds, portraits, painting and drawing courses. **Pangolino Tulipano**
pangolino@damanhur.it - Tel. + 39 347 4537930
Trompe l'oeil, portraits, waterpaintings, dream signs.
Ape Soja - Tel. + 39 320 7677902 - laoptah@gmail.com

"COBRA ALLORO" Sculpture

Statues. Sculptural portraits. Columns. Fountains.
Mexican stoves. Artistic fireplaces. Personalized gifts.
Sculpture classes. Stone restoration.
www.sculturaerestauro.it - teosimone@gmail.com
cobra@damanhur.it - Tel. + 39 348 5155710.

"AURIFOLIA" Art restoration

Methods of intervention that are ever more ethical and ecological. Courses.
www.aurifoliarestauri.it - info@aurifoliarestauri.it
Tel. +39 328 9896331 - Fax +39 0125 789738.

"HOBBIT MARGHERITA" Painter

Portraits, decorations, commissioned paintings, tromp l'oeil on canvas and walls.
hobbit@damanhur.it - Tel. +39 320 4780923.

"AythyA" Hand-painted silk

Dresses, scarves, umbrellas and accessories.
Refinement and uniqueness.
www.aythya-creazioni.it
aythya@damanhur.it - Tel. +39 320 4781900.

"OPUSSUM SPINACIO" Painter
Painting and art restoration.
opossum@damanhur.it - Tel. +39 329 9171902.

"LAOSEL" Iron art by Roberto Zurlo
Hand-crafted wrought iron.
Via Pramarzo 8, Baldissero Canavese
laosel@damanhur.com
Tel. +39 0124 512804 - Cel. +39 347 7671926.

WHERE TO HEAL WITH INTEGRATIVE MEDICINE

CASA DELLA SALUTE
Center for Integrative Medicine
Acupuncture and traditional Chinese medicine,
pain management, mental health, allergy treatments,
nutrition, dentistry, general ultrasound, ecodoppler,
orthoptics, mesotherapy, nursing services, general surgery.
www.creasalute.it
info@creasalute.it - Tel. +39 0125 789966.

"FISIOCREA" Private physiokinesitherapy center
Mind-body rehabilitation, functional rehabilitation,
massage therapy - gianluca@damanhur.it
Tel. +39 0125 789922 - +39 0125 789923.

WHERE TO RECEIVE WELLNESS AND BEAUTY TREATMENTS

"KYTHERA" with Nepa Citronella
Beauty pranatherapy, energetic balancing, stiloself, relaxing Selfica massage, steam bed with detoxifying mud, anti-gravity massage, Damanhurian self-massage.
kythera@kythera.it - Tel. +39 0125 791113.

"PERFORMA" Hairstyling for women and men
Eco-sustainable salon, with respect for hair and the environment.
Tel. +39 0125 791113 - +39 351 2116631
www.performastyle.it - facebook: performaecostyle

"ELA-SEL" experimental Selfica studio
New generation Selfs, stiloself, pranatherapy,
beauty pranatherapy, Damanhurian massage.
maia@damanhur.it - Tel. +39 348 8721720.

"FONOCROMO" Phono-cromo cabin
Treatments of sound, color and fragrances for wellness.
gau@damanhur.it - Tel. +39 328 3288850.

"MANABÀ" with Cincillà Ajucca
Naturopathy, flower therapy, herbal medicine, pranatherapy,
stiloself treatments, Essences of the Temples.
www.essenzedeltempio.com
info@essenzedeltempio.com - Tel. +39 349 2979721.

"CAVALLUCCIO MARINO ARNICA" Holistic Services
Naturopathy, spiritual healer, beauty pranatherapy,
Damanhurian and Selfic massage, Selfic treatments,
Mind Chess, Heartfelt Touch, reflexology.
Tel. +39 329 5379424 - rosemarieschade@hotmail.com

"CALABRONE" Holistic Services
Spiritual healer, craniosacral, Damanhurian treatments.
calabrone@damanhur.it - Tel. +39 347 5429402.

"TUCANO" Holistic Services
Counseling, pranatherapy, shiatsu, Selfic treatments.
tucano@damanhur.it - Tel. +39 339 3088436.

"SETTER G. J." Holistic Services
Trainer, Certified S.I.A.F.
(Società Italiana Armonizzatori Familiari)
Creator of the Heartfelt Touch and Mind Chess methods.
furfaro.antonino@gmail.com - Tel. +39 335 6657266.

"PERLA DONNA ASSOCIATION"
Consultation and courses in pregnancy, preparing for childbirth, sexuality, menopause and rehabilitation of the perineum.
Via Vittorio Emanuele 27 - Vidracco (TO).
Tel. +39 329 8375259 - +39 388 8275585.

WHERE TO FIND SELFS, SELFIC PAINTINGS AND SELFIC JEWELRY

"SELET" Selfic object studio and store
Objects and bracelets in copper with functions of energetic support for the individual and the environment.
www.sel-et.com - selet@damanhur.com
Tel. +39 0125 791144.

"NIATEL" Art Gallery
Permanent exhibition of Selfic paintings by Falco Tarassaco. Magical paintings, the magic of painting.
www.quadriselfici.it
info@quadriselfici.it - Tel. +39 389 1465831.

"OROCREA" Artistic Selfica jewelry

Jewelry art masterpieces.
www.orocrea.com - info@orocrea.com
Tel. +39 0125 789916.

WHERE TO FIND PRODUCTS AND SOLUTIONS FOR ECOLOGICAL AND SUSTAINABLE LIVING

"SOLERÀ" Renewable energy – Music of the Plants
Photovoltaics, electrical systems, solar thermal, heat pumps, biomass heaters (design and installation).
www.solera.info - solera@solera.info
Tel. +39 0125 789940 - Fax +39 0125 791005.

"SOLIOS" with Christine Schneider (Capra Carruba)
Green building consultant. Healthiness indoors
Materiali ecosostenibili - info@solios.eu
www.happyandhealthyliving.it - Tel. +39 348 4030717.

"EDILARCA"

Eco-sustainable and biocompatible construction & services
Sales of eco-building materials and FalFioc® producers, machines for blowing LACELLULOSA® in flakes.
www.lacellulosa.com - www.falfioc.com
info@edilarca.com - Tel. e Fax +39 0125 789683
Cell. +39 329 1297225.

"InAugeIniziative" Engineering company
Working mainly in the areas of fashion,
hotels and tourism, residential spaces and offices.
Specialized in green building - www.inaugeiniziative.it
info@inaugeiniziative.it - Tel. +39 0125 789772
Fax +39 0125 789877.

"RAMIL" Technical studio
Design and project management,
consulting and land registry, site safety (D.Lgs.81/08),
fire prevention, appraisals, energy certifications.
varano@damanhur.it - idra@damanhur.it
Tel. +39 328 9868877 - +39 320 0627166.

WHERE TO FIND OTHER PRODUCTS AND SERVICES

"FINETHIC", ethical insurance services
Cars, houses, condominiums, accidents, illness, organizations, businesses, professionals, securities, life insurance.
www.finethic.it - skype: segreteria.finethic
Tel. +39 0125 789713 - +39 329 2220285.

"MAKLERADO", Internet, mobile phone services, marketing. Design and development of web applications, e-learning systems and iOS and Android applications.
www.maklerado.it - info@maklerado.it

"DEVODAMA" marketing and communications, publishing, web development, multimedia - **www.devodama.it**
info@devodama.it - +39 0125 789645.

"CO.N.A.C.R.E.I.S." Social promotion organization
Conacreis is the first network of organizations in ethical, inner and spiritual research in Italy - **www.conacreis.it**
segreteria@conacreis.it - Tel. +39 0125 789773.

"COMPAGNIA DEI CARAIBI"
Prestigious importing company and distributor of luxury spirits from around the world. Carlo Alberto Reserve: vermouth, wine and spirits. Historical liqueurs, products from the founding of Damanhur - **Tel. + 39 0125 791104 - +39 348 1332805**
Via Marconi 8, Vidracco - **www.compagniadeicaraibi.com**

"VIVAIO DELLE NAIADI" with Naiade Corniolo
Edible wild plants and herbs. Plants for bees and butterflies.
www.vivaionaiadi.blogspot.com
info@vivaiodellenaiadi.com - Tel. +39 329 3945180.

AQUA IGNIS plumber and tinsmith
Mamba Iperico - **mamba@damanhur.it - +39 348 5601819.**

AROUND DAMANHUR

Damanhur is found in an area that has a lot of interesting variety in the nature and landscapes, full of art and tradition. Visiting Damanhur is an occasion to get to know the Canavase area of Italy too, a land that is very reserved and also capable of surprising you.

For nature lovers, an hour by car from Damanhur at Ceresole Reale, you find one of the entrances to the Gran Paradiso nature park, land of many animals, such as the ibex, chamois and marmot. There are excursions for "all kinds of legs," from the most demanding ones to reach the Alpine lakes, to more relaxed ones, close to the park facilities and buildings.

A half an hour drive from Damanhur is the Lago di Candia (Candia Lake) park, where there are also a variety of experiences, from hikes into the protected lake areas to relaxation time in the equipped zones. The organization that manages visits to Candia Lake also coordinates the Center for Documentation on the Monti Pelati, a protected hilly area adjacent to Damjl, which is also interesting to visit for its morphological peculiarities.

Going from Damanhur to the beginning of the Valchiusella area, you can reach Fondo.

From there, you can go on enthralling hikes along the river, through waterfalls and ruins of ancient villages, in a landscape that gradually becomes more silent and sparse of trees. In the area of Fondo and Traversella, you can find the "Sentiero delle Anime" (Path of Souls) where many rocks are marked with engravings and petroglyphs dating back to an uncertain period between the Neolithic and Bronze Age.

About 12 kilometers from Damanhur is the city of Ivrea. Ivrea is a center with notable initiatives in the cultural and artistic fields, in addition to being an active commercial city. Every year, it hosts the very famous Carnival celebration, the "Carnevale delle Arance" (Carnival of the Oranges), where for three days, the city districts invoke exploits of the resistance to Napoleon's troops with battles, launching oranges between teams. The Carnival attracts thousands of tourists from all over Europe every year. Ivrea stops for a few days, and the city "closes" while dedicating itself to this exciting challenge.

Also, about an hour by car from Damanhur is Turin, the Olympic city, the first Italian capital city, with nearby Caselle airport. A little less than an hour drive, you can reach Aosta in the heart of the Aosta Valley, at the foothills of the great "Monte Bianco" (Mont Blanc).

CON TE

"Con te" (in Italian, short for "I am with you") is the salutation that Damanhurians use to address other citizens, friends and guests. It is also our salutation at the end of this short guide. You may find more information on our websites, which you can access through our website **www.damanhur.org**.

In this book, we have condensed the essential information. Damanhur is many other things: emotions, activities, projects, making an effort every day to be a little better than the day before.

The conclusion to this can only be: "Come and visit us! Con te".

www.ingramcontent.com/pod-product-compliance
Lightning Source LLC
LaVergne TN
LVHW010315070426
835510LV00024B/3392